Animal Actors

by Katie Clark

Consultant:
Bonnie V. Beaver
College of Veterinary Medicine
Texas A&M University

BEARPORT PUBLISHING

New York, New York

Credits

Cover and Title Page, © Fuse/Thinkstock and © iStockphoto/Thinkstock; 4–5, © Paws for Effect; 6–7, © Ingram Publishing/Thinkstock; 8–9, © Carol Rosen; 10, © E. Spek/Shutterstock; 11, © iStockphoto/Thinkstock; 12–13, © Patrick Pleul/dpa/picture-alliance/Newscom; 14–15, © Idols/Photoshot/Newscom; 16–17, © Scott Barbour/Getty Images; 18–19, © cynoclub/Shutterstock; 20–21, © Paws for Effect; 22T, © Scott Barbour/Getty Images; 22C, © Anke van Wyk/Shutterstock; 22B, © Patrick Pleul/dpa/picture-alliance/Newscom; 23T, 23C, 23B, © Carol Rosen.

Publisher: Kenn Goin
Senior Editor: Joyce Tavolacci
Creative Director: Spencer Brinker
Design: Craig Hinton
Photo Researcher: Arnold Ringstad

Library of Congress Cataloging-in-Publication Data

Clark, Katie, 1962–
  Animal actors / by Katie Clark ; consultant, Bonnie V. Beaver.
    p. cm. — (We work!: Animals with jobs)
  Includes bibliographical references and index.
  ISBN-13: 978-1-61772-897-6 (library binding) — ISBN-10: 1-61772-897-7 (library binding)
  1. Animals in motion pictures—Juvenile literature. 2. Animals on television—Juvenile literature. I. Beaver, Bonnie V. G., 1944- II. Title.
  PN1995.9.A5C53 2014
  791.43'662—dc23
                          2013011500

For more information, write to Bearport Publishing Company, Inc., 45 West 21st Street, Suite 3B, New York, New York 10010. Printed in the United States of America.

10 9 8 7 6 5 4 3 2 1

Contents

Rex the Acting Dog

The **director** shouts, "Action!"

Rex pokes his head out of a car window and barks.

Then the director calls, "Cut."

Rex's **trainer** gives him a treat.

What is going on?

Rex is an animal actor playing a part in a movie!

Rex

Animals That Act

There are many different kinds of animal actors.

Dogs, horses, and pigs have all acted in movies and on TV.

Even elephants and bears have worked as actors.

One of the biggest animal actors was Keiko the killer whale in the movie *Free Willy*!

Keiko the killer whale

Acting Jobs

Animals can have many types of acting jobs.

They work in movies, on TV, and on the stage.

Like human actors, they play different parts.

Unlike human actors, however, animals always work with a trainer.

Trainers teach the animals what to do and when to do it.

8

Trainers

Animal actors learn to follow **commands** from their trainers.

The trainers first teach the animals simple tricks, such as roll over.

horse doing a trick

Once the animals learn the tricks, they get treats!

Then it is time for harder tricks.

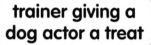

trainer giving a dog actor a treat

Quiet on the Set

Usually trainers teach animal actors spoken commands.

These include "sit," "stay," and "lie down."

However, some **movie sets** need to be kept very quiet.

Instead of speaking commands, trainers then use silent hand motions.

For example, a trainer might wave his hand when he wants a dog to bark.

trainer
using hand
motions

13

Wranglers

Dog actors can learn to run, jump, or growl on **cue**.

They can cover their eyes with their paws and do other funny tricks.

However, some animals, such as snakes, cannot follow commands.

They have wranglers instead of trainers.

Wranglers handle and control the animals during filming.

14

movie director

snake wrangler

15

Finding Work

Just like human actors, animal actors **audition** for roles.

Directors want to see how the animals look and behave.

They also want to know if the animals can follow commands.

Staying Safe

In some movies, animals perform daring tricks.

For example, a dog might have to leap from a car.

A horse might have to balance on its back legs.

Luckily, trainers teach the animals how to do these things safely.

Animal Stars

Animal actors have exciting jobs.

However, it takes a lot of hard work to be an actor.

Thanks to their trainers, many animal actors are great performers.

Who knows—the next big movie star might have fur and a tail!

Glossary

audition
(aw-DISH-uhn)
to try getting an
acting job

commands
(kuh-MANDZ)
orders given by
someone to do
something

cue (KYOO)
a signal to
do something

director
(duh-REK-tur)
a person who
tells actors what
to do

movie sets
(MOO-vee SETS)
large rooms or
outdoor areas where
movies are made

trainer (TRAY-nur)
a person who teaches
an animal actor how
to perform

23

Index

Read More

Helfer, Ralph. *The World's Greatest Lion.* New York: Philomel Books (2012).

Whitehead, Sarah. *How to Speak Dog.* New York: Scholastic (2008).

Learn More Online

To learn more about animal actors, visit
www.bearportpublishing.com/WeWork

About the Author

Katie Clark has written many books, articles, and apps for children. She enjoys spending time reading, writing, and playing make-believe with her daughters.